SPORTS STARS WITH HEART

Shaquille O'Neal
GIANT ON AND OFF THE COURT

by Tom Robinson

Enslow Publishers, Inc.
40 Industrial Road
Box 398
Berkeley Heights, NJ 07922
USA
http://www.enslow.com

Library of Congress Cataloging-in-Publication Data
Robinson, Tom.
  Shaquille O'Neal : giant on and off the court / Tom Robinson. — 1st ed.
    p. cm. — (Sports stars with heart)
  Includes bibliographical references and index.
  ISBN 0-7660-2823-2
  1. O'Neal, Shaquille—Juvenile literature. 2. Basketball players—United
States—Biography—Juvenile literature. I. Title. II. Series.
  GV884.O54R63 2006
  796.323092—dc22   2006012546

Credits
Editorial Direction: Red Line Editorial, Inc. (Bob Temple)
Editor: Sue Green
Designer: Lindaanne Donohoe

Printed in the United States of America

10 9 8 7 6 5 4 3 2 1

To Our Readers: We have done our best to make sure all Internet
addresses in this book were active and appropriate when we went to press.
However, the author and the publisher have no control over and assume no
liability for the material available on those Internet sites or on other Web
sites they may link to. Any comments or suggestions can be sent by e-mail
to comments@enslow.com or to the address on the back cover.

Photographs © 2006: AP Photo/Elise Amendola: 56; AP Photo/Tim Boyle: 52;
AP Photo/Duane Burleson: 13; AP Photo/Alan Diaz: 16, 97; AP Photo/Kevork
Djansezian: 63, 71, 77; AP Photo/Ric Francis: 103; AP Photo/Bill Haber: 20; AP
Photo/John Hick: 3, 27; AP Photo/Mark Humphrey: 37; AP photo/Bill Kostroun:
45; AP Photo/Adrees Latif: 84–85; AP Photo/Mark Lennihan: 49; AP Photo/Miami
Beach Police Department: 68; AP Photo/Steve Mitchell: 106; AP Photo/ Lucy
Nicholson: 92–93; AP Photo/David J. Phillip: cover, 1, 3; AP Photo/Chris Pizzello:
4; AP Photo/Don Ryan: 3, 42; AP Photo/Lynne Sladky: 11; AP Photo/ Mark J.
Terrill: 19; AP Photo/Nick Ut: 73; AP Photo/Bill Waugh: 31; AP Photo/ Steve C.
Wilson: 60

Cover Photo: The Miami Heat's Shaquille O'Neal dunks the ball in a game
against the Rockets January 29, 2006, in Houston.

C O N T E N T S

Artists fill in a mural of Shaq on a building in Los Angeles.

CHAPTER ONE

Happy in Miami

National Basketball Association Commissioner David Stern stood before the media October 29, 1996, at the Grand Hyatt Hotel in New York City. With the league celebrating its fiftieth anniversary, Stern unveiled the list of the 50 Greatest Players in NBA History.

Players from the early years of the league were honored. There were many stars who helped the league grow into its worldwide fame in the late 1970s and early 1980s. Michael Jordan, Karl Malone, and Patrick Ewing gave the list some active players in their thirties who had established their place in the game in the last decade or more.

There was one player whose place on the list stood out—stood out in the way that only an athletic and

THE 50 GREATEST PLAYERS IN NBA HISTORY

Kareem Abdul-Jabbar	Karl Malone
Nate Archibald	Moses Malone
Paul Arizin	Pete Maravich
Charles Barkley	Kevin McHale
Rick Barry	George Mikan
Elgin Baylor	Earl Monroe
Dave Bing	Hakeem Olajuwon
Larry Bird	Shaquille O'Neal
Wilt Chamberlain	Robert Parish
Bob Cousy	Bob Pettit
Dave Cowens	Scottie Pippen
Billy Cunningham	Willis Reed
Dave DeBusschere	Oscar Robertson
Clyde Drexler	David Robinson
Julius Erving	Bill Russell
Patrick Ewing	Dolph Schayes
Walt Frazier	Bill Sharman
George Gervin	John Stockton
Hal Greer	Isiah Thomas
John Havlicek	Nate Thurmond
Elvin Hayes	Wes Unseld
Magic Johnson	Bill Walton
Sam Jones	Jerry West
Michael Jordan	Lenny Wilkens
Jerry Lucas	James Worthy

SOURCE: NBA announcement, October 29, 1996.

powerful, seven-foot one-inch, 325-pound man can. Shaquille O'Neal, at just twenty-four years old, was by far the youngest player on the list. Easily recognized simply as "Shaq," O'Neal had already made a name for himself in the first four seasons of his NBA career as a member of the Orlando Magic.

Shaq was just starting a successful run as center of the Los Angeles Lakers when the list was announced. He was only beginning to put together the type of career that now places him among the best to ever play his position.

As an imposing force in the middle, Shaq teamed with Kobe Bryant to lead the Lakers to three straight NBA titles in 2000, 2001, and 2002.

It was often debated who was the most important Laker. Was it Shaq, for his scoring and physical presence rebounding and defending inside? Or was it Bryant, for his outside scoring and ability to shut down an opponent's top individual scorer?

SHAQUILLE O'NEAL

Born: March 6, 1972, in Newark, N.J.

Height: 7' 1"

Weight: 325 pounds

Team: Miami Heat

Previous Teams: Orlando Magic, Los Angeles Lakers

Position: Center

Off the Court: Is active in many community organizations and has his own charitable foundation, the Real Model Foundation. His stardom extends to being an actor in movies and a rapper in the music industry.

Each time the Lakers won a championship, however, it was Shaq who walked away as the NBA Finals' Most Valuable Player.

TIME FOR A CHANGE

By the time the Lakers lost to the Detroit Pistons in the 2004 NBA Finals, Shaq was unhappy. His relationship with Bryant had deteriorated. It was clear that for the Lakers to move forward, they would have to choose between two powerful personalities.

When the Lakers decided to build around the younger Bryant, it was time for Shaq to prove himself elsewhere. The Miami Heat sent three players and a future first-round draft pick to the Lakers for Shaq. When he arrived in Miami, Shaq immediately connected with another up-and-coming guard to build a formidable one-two punch on the court.

SHAQUILLE O'NEAL'S CAREER NBA TRANSACTIONS

June 24, 1992: **First overall pick in NBA Draft by the Orlando Magic.**

July 18, 1996: **Signed as a free agent by the Los Angeles Lakers.**

July 14, 2004: **Acquired by the Miami Heat from the Los Angeles Lakers in a trade for Caron Butler, Brian Grant, Lamar Odom, and a first-round draft pick.**

Shaq and Dwayne Wade became a combination the Eastern Conference had a hard time stopping. The Heat went all the way to the conference final in 2005, their first year together, before winning the franchise's first NBA championship in 2006.

The Heat's first championship almost came sooner. Miami was giving Detroit trouble in the 2005 Eastern Conference Finals when Wade suffered a rib injury. Shaq, already slowed by a thigh injury, and Wade did their best to play hurt, but the Heat could not hold on in its final game against the Pistons.

The Lakers faltered and missed the playoffs in the first season after Shaq left Los Angeles. Miami had been out of the playoffs in 2002 and 2003 before reaching the second round in 2004. Shaq was universally recognized for lifting his new team even higher and finished as runner-up in voting for the league's regular-season MVP award.

DID YOU KNOW?
When Shaquille O'Neal sat out two games of the 2005 second-round playoff series against the Washington Wizards, it was the first time in his career that he missed a playoff game. He had appeared in 164 straight playoff games before the bruised right thigh sidelined him for Game 3 and Game 4.

"We just had a phenomenal season," Shaq said. "Everybody fought. Guys played well. We almost had it."[1]

Charles Barkley, one of the NBA's 50 Greatest Players and a television commentator for Turner Sports, explained the differences in the two teams.

"Everybody is better when they play with Shaquille O'Neal," Barkley told reporters before the 2005 All-Star Game. "I mean look at this thing there. We haven't heard anything from Devean George, Derek Fisher. Rick Fox retired. All those guys are good players, but they are not nearly as good without Shaquille. We did not even know that Damon Jones was alive until two months ago. Now he is leading the league in three-point shooting. Why? Because his man is camped in Shaquille O'Neal's lap all night. Great players make good guys around them better."[2]

> **"Everybody is better when they play with Shaquille O'Neal."**
>
> **—Charles Barkley**

When the Heat came within a game of the NBA Finals, the finish left the team encouraged. Heat management went out in the off-season and added players to the Shaq-Wade combination in order to pursue a championship.

Miami Heat coach Pat Riley talks with Shaq before a game against the Atlanta Hawks on December 20, 2005.

When the 2005–06 season started a little slowly, coach Stan Van Gundy resigned to spend more time with his family. That opened up a spot on the bench for Pat Riley to come down from the Heat front office and resume a legendary coaching career. Just as Shaq, Kobe Bryant, and coach Phil Jackson had led a run in Los Angeles, Shaq, Wade, and Riley were now ready to build a similar situation in Miami.

Three months after Shaq turned thirty-four—and 10 years after Stern's announcement—Shaq won his fourth NBA title. The championship began materializing before Riley moved to the bench. Riley made a series of offseason moves to get Shaq and Wade help.

"I think Pat is getting Laker flashbacks," Shaq said, "because all the teams he won championships with, they had a one-two punch, but they also had some great players with them. That's what we need, because if one or two of our guys get hurt and we get to a Game 7, we need somebody of that caliber who can step up."[3]

As the Lakers learned, the Heat were much tougher in big games with the combination of Shaq and an explosive young guard. Not every team gets to build around one of the NBA's all-time greatest players.

"Dwyane Wade . . . is going to be a better player playing with Shaquille O'Neal."

—Charles Barkley

The way Barkley saw it, the chance to play with Shaq was a perfect opportunity for Wade, who became an all-star in his second season in the NBA—and his first with Shaq as a teammate. A year later, Wade was the MVP of the NBA Finals.

Shaq takes it on the chin from Detroit's Ben Wallace while driving to the basket.

"Dwayne Wade is a really good player but he is going to be a better player playing with Shaquille O'Neal because he is going to get easier drives to the basket," Barkley said in the aftermath of the trade that sent Shaq to Miami. "Shaquille O'Neal's man is not going to leave him. So that gives him another step or two to finish at the basket, or have an area to work in. Something that simple means a lot to players. Shaquille O'Neal's man can't leave him. And that little post-up difference is the difference between getting a dunk or layup and having to shoot a tough floater. It's a big difference."[4]

Wade proved Barkley correct. With Shaq's help, the all-star guard was a dominating force on the league's best team when the 2005–06 season ended.

The Magic, Lakers, and Heat have seen that the way Shaq changes play in the paint can be the difference between fighting to make the playoffs and playing for NBA championships.

CHAPTER TWO

Moving Here
and There

Shaquille O'Neal has a simple answer when asked about where home is. "Home is where my mother is," Shaq says.[1] Ask Lucille O'Neal Harrison, Shaq's mother, and the answer is equally simple. "Home is wherever we're living," she says.[2]

As an adult, Shaq seems right at home in so many places. When Hurricane Katrina hit Louisiana hard in 2005, Shaq was one of the celebrities who helped people who were once among his fans when he played there in college. He fit in immediately in Orlando, where he began his professional career.

Shaq helps load a truck with donations for victims of Hurricane Katrina September 8, 2005, in Miami.

Shaq seemed right at home in Hollywood as a celebrity athlete, actor, and musician. Now back in Florida as a member of the Miami Heat, Shaq again appears comfortable in his surroundings.

Playing basketball in three cities during his professional career has been no great shock to Shaq's way of life. At least each of the major changes in his basketball career took place during the off-season. That gave Shaq time to prepare for and adjust to his new scenery.

SHAQUILLE O'NEAL'S BASKETBALL TRAVELS

1980s: Learned basketball while living in Germany

1987–89: Cole High School, San Antonio

1989–92: Louisiana State University

1992–96: Orlando Magic

1996–2004: Los Angeles Lakers

2004–: Miami Heat

Growing up in a military family, Shaq did not always have the chance to prepare himself for changes. And those changes were not necessarily during convenient times. By the time he was in sixth grade, Shaq was in his fifth school system—and on his second continent.

Shaq was born in Newark, N.J., in 1972. His mother, Lucille O'Neal, married Phillip Harrison when Shaq was two. Harrison started a career in the army and the family moved to a military base for the first time when Shaq was in first grade. The family remained in New Jersey but moved from Bayonne to Eatontown late in Shaq's third-grade year. When Shaq was halfway through fifth grade, the family moved to Fort Stewart in Georgia.

Each time Shaq arrived in a new town, there were adjustments to be made. He was always much bigger than other kids his age. They would want to know if he had failed a grade. If the questions and teasing led to a fight, it was easy for Shaq to give the impression of being big and scary. His mother even developed a habit of carrying his birth certificate to prove his age to strangers.

The adjustments were just beginning. In sixth grade, Harrison's newest assignment took him to Germany. Shaq rebelled early in his days in Germany, but his stepfather remained strict. He insisted on proper behavior, and Shaq learned his lesson. "When I think back to those early years of moving around, the times I was unhappy in various places, I can see the other side of the coin," Shaq wrote in an autobiography after his first NBA season.

FAMILY TIES
Mother: Lucille O'Neal Harrison
Stepfather: Phillip Harrison
Sisters: Ayesha and Lateefah
Brother: Jamal

Shaq and his stepfather, Phillip Harrison, celebrate the Lakers'
second straight NBA championship June 15, 2001, in Philadelphia.

"You learn things as an army brat that you don't even
know you're learning. The discipline, for one thing."[3]

Shaq's interest in basketball grew while he was in
Germany. That interest eventually changed his life. It
was a change his stepfather recognized as it was
developing. "You see this ball?" Phillip Harrison once
asked a young Shaq. "You take care of this ball, you
live with this ball, you sleep with this ball, you dream
with this ball. Because, someday this ball is going to
put food on the table."[4]

Shaq's mother, Lucille Harrison, hugs her son's former college coach, Dale Brown, after Shaq's graduation from Louisiana State University in 2000.

HOW OLD ARE YOU?

When Shaq's age was mistaken at a basketball clinic at the army base in Germany, the implications were much different. Louisiana State basketball coach Dale Brown was speaking at the clinic and gave Shaq the ball to take a shot at one point in a demonstration.

After the presentation, Shaq approached Brown for tips on strengthening his legs so he could jump better. He was already six-foot six-inches at thirteen years old but was unable to dunk. The coach told Shaq about Nautilus exercises that could strengthen his legs, and then asked the type of question that normally embarrassed the youngster: "How long you been in the army, soldier?"[5]

Brown just assumed from Shaq's size that he was an enlisted man. When he found out he was talking to a thirteen-year-old who had not yet played high school basketball, the coach made a point of meeting Shaq's stepfather before leaving the base.

Shaq kept working on his basketball moves in Germany. When his family returned to the United States, with an assignment in San Antonio, Shaq was ready to become a force in high school basketball and a top prospect for coaches such as Brown to watch.

CHAPTER THREE

Growing Up Shaq

Dave Madura coached basketball at Robert G. Cole Junior/Senior High School in San Antonio.

As part of the Fort Sam Houston Independent School District, teachers and coaches at Cole were used to students coming and going all the time. Their students were primarily the children of service people and Department of Defense workers who were often moved around the country.

Madura, however, was not accustomed to adding six-foot eight-inch, 230-pound sophomores to his program.

That is the gift he received when Shaq's family returned to the United States. Shaq enrolled at Cole in April of his sophomore year, but it was too late for basketball that season.

Football coach and athletic director Joel Smith also noticed Shaq. He sought out the new student but wound up only adding a dedicated statistician to his program. Shaq, who had dabbled in baseball and football a little when he was younger, had decided by then that basketball was the sport he wanted to pursue.

Adding a player of Shaq's physical ability can make an immediate impact at a small school. Cole was a 2-A school in Texas, where 5-A is the largest and A is the smallest, but moved up to play Class 3-A competition in Shaq's senior season.

ROBERT G. COLE JUNIOR/SENIOR HIGH SCHOOL

District: **Sam Houston Independent School District**

Jurisdiction: **The school district is subject to the rules and regulations of the state of Texas and the federal government. It is one of three military school districts in Texas, all of which are located in San Antonio.**

Who Attends: **Children of military personnel residing on the military reservations of Fort Sam Houston and Camp Bullis**

Enrollment: **As of 2005, there were 446 students in grades seven through twelve.**

"Very few coaches are fortunate enough to get a kid that big and talented."

—Dave Madura

With Shaq's game developing quickly, Cole immediately became a contender for a state championship.

"Very few coaches are fortunate enough to get a kid that big and talented," Madura said. "He was the catalyst, of course, but we had some other kids who did a great job that year, too."[1]

Madura realized his fortune, but he was not satisfied with just taking what Shaq was ready to add to the Cole program. Instead, the high school coach became one of the keys in developing the strong game that Shaq now uses to dominate the paint in the National Basketball Association. "I wanted him to get better, so I pushed him every day," Madura said.[2]

Current Cole coach Herb More, who was an assistant on Shaq's state championship team, said it was Madura's discipline that helped complete the development of the budding prospect's game. "Shaq told me several times that there are few coaches he's really respected for their discipline, and Dave is one he always has mentioned," More said. "Coach Madura didn't take any guff off anybody. He treated everybody the same."[3]

STEADY GROWTH

Sophomore year, arrival at Cole: 6' 8", 230 pounds
Junior basketball season: 6' 10", 250 pounds
Senior basketball season: 6' 11", 260 pounds

Shaq's first season at Cole featured 32 straight wins. The Cougars reached the Region IV Class 2-A final with ease. Their season, however, ended in disappointment. Playing Liberty Hill for the region title, Shaq found himself in immediate foul trouble. The game ended poorly as well with two key misses from the foul line in the closing seconds.

A hungrier Shaq made his impact on the summer basketball circuit to move up among the ranks of the nation's top recruits. The lessons Madura had been teaching were sinking in. Madura wanted his big man to think about power dunks instead of soft finesse moves around the basket that would allow opponents to grab his arms, sometimes sending him to the foul line, sometimes not getting called at all. "One day I realized that all those little misses when I got fouled would at least be two points if I dunked," Shaq said.[4]

COLLEGE BECKONS

Shaq headed to the Basketball Congress Invitational in Houston and outperformed higher-ranked recruits. He went to another tournament in Arizona and repeated the effort. Suddenly letters from major college recruiters were pouring in from all across the country. One of those recruiters was Dale Brown, the Louisiana State University coach whom Shaq and his father had met more than three years earlier in Germany.

Brown's dedication and persistence toward recruiting Shaq, even before others discovered him, paid off. Before Shaq's senior season started, he committed to a full basketball scholarship from LSU. Phillip Harrison even hung an LSU flag in front of their home to make it clear that Shaq's mind was made up.

All that was left to concentrate on was making up for the previous season's disappointment. Shaq was an unstoppable force, leading the Cougars to a perfect season. He blocked as many as 22 shots in one game. Shaq scored 52 points in one state tournament game. He finished the season averaging 32 points, 22 rebounds, and 8 blocked shots per game.

Madura was in tears as the final seconds ticked away and Shaq and his teammates celebrated a 66–60 victory against Clarksville in the Class 3-A state final.

Shaq shoots against the North in the gold medal game in 1990.

"I don't remember him ever missing a workout."

—Dave Madura

"I don't remember him ever missing a workout," Madura said. "Shaq wanted to win and he had a great work ethic. Whether it was on the basketball court or lifting weights, he worked hard."[5]

Once an unhappy youngster moving from one city to another, Shaq found happiness in San Antonio and at Cole. "I loved that school," he said. "I have flashbacks of how much fun it was every time I go back to visit."[6]

ABOUT SAN ANTONIO

Population: **1,144,646, according to the 2000 United States Census. Now more than 1.2 million, making it the second largest city in Texas and eighth largest in the United States**

Located: **Bexar County, south-central Texas**

Founded: **1718**

History: **In 1836, the Battle of the Alamo was fought in what was then the outskirts of the city and is now part of San Antonio**

Military connection: **In addition to Fort Sam Houston, Lackland Air Force Base, Randolph Air Force Base, and Brooks City Base are also located in the city**

The man who continued to mold Shaq's game during those important years acknowledges that, at the time, he was not so sure he was overseeing the development of one of the game's all-time greats. "I knew he could develop into a great one, but I didn't really think he would reach the heights he did," Madura said. "He just got so much bigger and stronger than I ever thought he would."[7]

In hindsight, the current status is a result of that work in high school. "San Antonio was where I first made my mark in the basketball world," Shaq said. "It was all struggles up until then."[8] However, it was all celebrations by the time he was ready to leave San Antonio.

The success in San Antonio meant there were more travels ahead. Shaq was ready to start chasing the national fame that goes with college and professional basketball stardom.

Shaq the Tiger

Shaquille O'Neal may not have been able to play a better college basketball game, and he knew it. But sitting in the locker room after what wound up being his final game at Louisiana State University, Shaq was only able to think about what he had not accomplished. Shaq ultimately decided to move on to professional basketball, and after an 89–79 loss to Indiana, he was thinking that he still had never made it to a Final Four.

"I've never been more ready to play a basketball game than I was that afternoon," Shaq wrote a year later.[1] Indeed, he had even conquered a career-long nemesis by making all 12 free throws. Playing against a team guided by Bobby Knight, one of the game's all-time great defensive coaches, Shaq scored 36 points.

Shaq hangs on the rim after a slam dunk in the Midwest Regionals.

CAREER COLLEGE STATISTICS

SEASON	YEAR	G	FG%	FT%
Freshman	1989–90	32	57.3	55.6
Sophomore	1990–91	28	62.8	63.8
Junior	1991–92	30	61.5	52.8
	Totals	90	61.0	57.5

He also grabbed 12 rebounds, blocked 5 shots, and even made a couple of steals.

Shaq had come a long way from the college freshman who was a force inside but still played second fiddle offensively to veteran guard Chris Jackson. He had become one of the dominant players in all of college basketball. Shaq was named national Player of the Year by The Associated Press, United Press International, and *Sports Illustrated* after his sophomore season, when he led the country in rebounds with 14.7 per game. When his junior season ended, he was a consensus All-American as one of the nation's top five players while leading the country with 5.3 blocked shots per game.

Despite all the success, the college game was growing frustrating. Shaq thought players were being allowed to manhandle him unnecessarily. And he knew a professional career was waiting.

PTS	AVG	REB AVG	AST	BLK	ST
445	13.9	12.0	61	115	38
774	27.6	14.7	45	140	41
722	24.1	14.0	46	157	29
1,941	21.6	13.5	152	412	108

KEY:
G — Games played
FG% — Field-goal percentage
FT% — Free-throw percentage
PTS — Points
AVG — Average points per game
REB AVG — Rebound average
AST — Assists
BLK — Blocked shots
ST — Steals

QUIET START

Shaq made a quiet debut in college basketball with 10 points and 5 rebounds in a 91–80 victory against Mississippi. After scoring 10 points in each of his first two games, Shaq went over 20 in his fourth and fifth games. While averaging 13.9 points in his freshman season, he established his all-around play. He was just as likely to put up big numbers on the boards as he was in the scoring column. Shaq pulled down a season-high 24 rebounds in an overtime win against Loyola Marymount and 21 against Kentucky.

The 1989–90 LSU season came to an end in the second round of the NCAA tournament—also known as March Madness. After beating Villanova 70–63 in the first round, the Tigers lost to Georgia Tech, 94–91, with Shaq scoring 19 points and grabbing 14 rebounds. LSU had been ranked as high as second in the country early in the season and did have a win against eventual national champion Nevada-Las Vegas, but they finished just 23–9 overall.

DID YOU KNOW?

Shaquille O'Neal graduated from Louisiana State University in December 2000. He received a bachelor's degree in general studies with a minor in political science.

Shaq was the LSU basketball team's top student each of his three years there. He had a 2.9 grade-point average—out of a possible 4.0—as a freshman. When he eventually left after his junior season, he had a GPA of 3.0. He was well on his way to the degree he would eventually earn.

The work in the classroom was part of what kept Shaq around beyond the end of his sophomore season. With LSU's offensive emphasis switched to getting the ball to its big man, Shaq quickly established himself as college basketball's top player that season.

CAREER NIGHT

Shaquille O'Neal's statistics against Arkansas State
December 18, 1990, in a 98–74 victory:

Field goals:	18
Field goals attempted:	26
Free throws:	17
Free throws attempted:	21
Points:	53
Rebounds:	19

That also made him the hottest prospect for the National Basketball Association and the likely first pick in the draft if he decided to turn pro right then.

PLAYER OF THE YEAR

Shaq started his sophomore season by scoring 24 points in a 93–91 loss to Villanova in a rematch of the NCAA tournament. When he broke out for a career-high 53 points in a 98–74 rout of Arkansas State in the sixth game of the season, Shaq's scoring average soared to 29.7 points per game. He was not finished. Shaq had eight more games with at least 30 points. However, he missed two games with a hairline fracture in his leg late in the season.

Shaq returned in time for the NCAA tournament. He overcame any potential problems with his leg to score 27 points and grab 16 rebounds against Connecticut. The Tigers, however, fell short, and their tournament ended in just one game, with a 79–62 loss to the Huskies.

Many factors went into deciding whether to stay in college. Both Shaq and his stepfather believed he was on the receiving end of unnecessarily rough and illegal tactics that could lead to more injuries. A promise to his mother that he would use his basketball scholarship to graduate from college was one of the big reasons that kept Shaq from walking away at that point.

With the returning national Player of the Year back in the lineup, there were high expectations for LSU entering the 1991–92 season. After a disappointing 3–3 start, the Tigers won ten of their next eleven games, with Shaq averaging 29 points and 17.4 rebounds in that stretch. Consecutive losses to Duke, Georgia, and Vanderbilt slowed the momentum, but LSU's only loss in the final six regular-season games came in overtime.

The Tigers went into the postseason on a roll. Then, a fight broke out in LSU's Southeastern Conference tournament game with Tennessee. Shaq drew an automatic suspension for the next game, and the Tigers lost to Kentucky.

Shaq wrestles with Carlus Groves (33) of the University of Tennessee during the Southeastern Conference Tournament March 13, 1992.

Back again for the NCAA tournament's West Regional, Shaq had 26 points and 13 rebounds in a 94–83 win against Brigham Young. That was only part of the story. Shaq blocked 11 shots, the most ever in one game in the tournament.

The Tigers and their big man seemed sharp, but despite one of Shaq's best games, the championship dream ended March 21, 1992, with the loss to Indiana.

MARCH MADNESS

Shaquille O'Neal's NCAA Tournament History

OPPONENT	YEAR	RESULT	FG–FGA	FT–FTA	POINTS	REB
Villanova	1990	Won, 70–63	4–8	4–7	12	11
Georgia Tech	1990	Lost, 94–91	5–10	9–12	19	14
Connecticut	1991	Lost, 79–62	11–22	5–6	27	16
Brigham Young	1992	Won, 94–83	11–17	4–7	26	13
Indiana	1992	Lost, 89–79	12–18	12–12	36	12
Totals		Won 2, Lost 3	43–75	34–44	120	66
Percent/Average			57.3	77.3	24.0	13.2

KEY:
FG–FGA — Field goals made–Field goals attempted
FT–FTA — Free throws made–Free throws attempted
REB — Rebounds

In his autobiography, *Shaq Attaq!*, Shaq described a drive home from campus in Baton Rouge to San Antonio late one night not long after the loss to Indiana. During that drive, he made up his mind that it was time to leave college. At home, he talked it over with his parents and moved on. After calling coach Dale Brown at LSU, Shaq set up a press conference in San Antonio and announced that he was declaring his eligibility for the NBA Draft.

"The college game really isn't made for seven-foot centers. They can triple-team you, foul you intentionally, and the refs just don't have much sympathy."

—Shaquille O'Neal

"The college game really isn't made for seven-foot centers," Shaq said. "They can triple-team you, foul you intentionally, and the refs just don't have much sympathy.

"They say, 'Hey, he can take it, because he's big,' as if that should have anything to do with it. I don't think in the NFL they let guys clip Bruce Smith just because he's a big tough defensive end. Rules are rules, or they're supposed to be."[2]

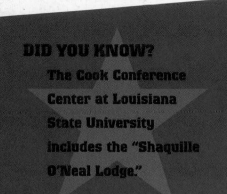

NBA opponents certainly did not take a hands-off approach to defending Shaq, but in the years ahead he showed the professional game was made for his abilities.

BEFORE, DURING, AND AFTER

LSU in three seasons before Shaquille O'Neal arrived:	60–41
LSU in three seasons with Shaquille O'Neal:	63–29
LSU in three seasons after Shaquille O'Neal left:	45–42

CHAPTER FIVE

Magic 5 Times

The Orlando Magic had been around for just three years and were coming off a 21–61 record in the 1991–92 season when they found themselves with the first pick in the National Basketball Association Draft. Shaquille O'Neal just happened to have made himself available for that draft when he decided to leave Louisiana State University after his junior season. Shaq soon had his own Magic Kingdom after being selected by the team that gets its name from nearby Disney World.

Teams that miss the NBA playoffs wind up in a lottery for a chance to have the first pick in the draft. As the second-worst team in the league, the Magic had the second-best chance of winning the lottery.

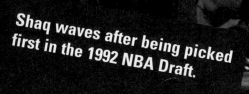

Shaq waves after being picked first in the 1992 NBA Draft.

Orlando's luck held up with a lottery win May 17, 1992. That off-court win is still described as "The Most Important Day in Franchise History" in a story on the team's Web site.

There were a few formalities to be taken care of, but the Magic were able to instantly look forward to better times after winning eighteen, thirty-one, and twenty-one games in their first three seasons in the NBA. Rumors and speculation suggested possible trades or other alternatives, but Orlando held on to its pick and used it to add Shaq.

FIRST 10 PICKS, 1992 NBA DRAFT

	NBA Team	Player	College
1.	Orlando Magic	Shaquille O'Neal	Louisiana State
2.	Charlotte Hornets	Alonzo Mourning	Georgetown
3.	Minnesota Timberwolves	Christian Laettner	Duke
4.	Dallas Mavericks	Jimmy Jackson	Ohio State
5.	Denver Nuggets	LaPhonso Ellis	Notre Dame
6.	Washington Bullets	Tom Gugliotta	North Carolina State
7.	Sacramento Kings	Walt Williams	Maryland
8.	Milwaukee Bucks	Todd Day	Arkansas
9.	Philadelphia 76ers	Clarence Weatherspoon	Southern Mississippi
10.	Atlanta Hawks	Adam Keefe	Stanford

"If we display the type of teamwork we displayed during negotiations, we should be able to make something happen in Orlando."

—Shaquille O'Neal

Large contract negotiations seldom are easy, but Shaq and his agent, Leonard Amato, were able to work things out with the Magic and owner Rich DeVos by early August. Shaq signed for seven years and more than $40 million in what was believed to be the largest contract ever for a rookie in any professional sport. "If we display the type of teamwork we displayed during negotiations, we should be able to make something happen in Orlando," Shaq said during the press conference to announce his signing.[1]

Shaq was also busy with endorsement deals, including a large one with Pepsi that would bring in more money. After wearing uniform number 33 in college, Shaq hoped to do the same with the Magic. Terry Catledge, however, was already wearing number 33 for Orlando. After discussions about a possible change, Shaq backed off later in August and announced he would be wearing number 32. "They were saying I was the spoiled rookie and Terry

Pat Williams, president and general manager of the Magic, holds up a jersey with O'Neal's name after winning the NBA lottery.

Catledge was the veteran forward being forced to give up his number," Shaq said. "Well, it was never that way."[2]

IMMEDIATE IMPACT

With a contract and a uniform in his possession, Shaq was ready to get started. Unlike the early days at LSU, he made an immediate impact, instantly making it clear what the Magic were getting for their considerable investment.

The speed and style with which NBA teams double-teamed caused Shaq some early problems, but he gave defenses fits as well. Shaq tried to learn how and where to pass to work the ball away from double teams. However, he turned the ball over 9 times in his first professional exhibition game and 8 times in his first regular-season game. That was about the only negative statistic. Shaq had 25 points in his first exhibition game. He scored 12 points and grabbed 18 rebounds in his first official game.

Shaq became the first rookie ever named NBA Player of the Week in his first week in the league. From the start, Shaq was able to compete with the league's best and most established players. Clearly, he was the best rookie, not just that season, but to come into the league in many years. In fact, Shaq was the first rookie since Michael Jordan—eight years earlier—to be voted into a starting spot in the NBA All-Star Game.

Shaq was selected as the NBA's Rookie of the Month for four straight months. Shaq's average of 23.4 points, 13.9 rebounds, and 3.5 blocks per game

NBA ALL-STAR GAME
Shaquille O'Neal's All-Star Statistics

TEAM	YEAR	MINUTES	FG–FGA	FT–FTA	POINTS	REB
East	1993	25	4–9	6–9	14	7
East	1994	26	2–12	4–11	8	10
East	1995	26	9–16	4–7	22	7
East	1996	28	10–16	5–11	25	10
West	1998	18	5–10	2–4	12	4
West	2000	25	11–20	0–2	22	9
West	2003	26	8–14	3–5	19	13
West	2004	24	12–19	0–1	24	11
East	2005	26	6–11	0–3	12	6
East	2006	23	7-9	3-5	17	9
TOTALS		247	74-136	27-58	175	86
AVERAGES/PERCENTS		24.7	54.4	46.6	17.5	8.6

KEY:
FG–FGA — Field goals made–attempted
FT–FTA — Free throws made–attempted
REB — Rebounds

and his field goal percentage of 56.2 were the best among all rookies. He finished second in the entire league in rebounds and blocked shots while ranking fourth in shooting percentage and eighth in scoring. Nobody else in the league ranked in the top ten in all four categories. When it came time for sports writers and broadcasters to select the Rookie of the Year, Shaq won in a runaway, getting 96 of the 98 first-place votes. Charlotte center Alonzo Mourning received the other two.

The Magic improved 20 games to a 41–41 record. When he received the Rookie of the Year award, Shaq was already looking ahead to better times. "I hope I can get an NBA championship trophy to go along with it," Shaq said, "so that when I retire and have children, I can tell my son, 'I was bad.'"[3]

> "I hope I can get an NBA championship trophy to go along with it, so that when I retire and have children, I can tell my son, 'I was bad.'"
>
> —Shaquille O'Neal

Charles Smith tries to keep Shaq away from a rebound.

The Orlando Magic's record with Shaquille O'Neal, as well as before he joined the team and after he left it:

Before Shaq

1989–90	18–64
1990–91	31–51
1991–92	21–61

With Shaq

1992–93	41–41
1993–94	50–32
1994–95	57–25
1995–96	60–22

After Shaq

1996–97	45–37
1997–98	41–41
1998–99	33–17
1999–2000	41–41

COMING CLOSE

The Magic won 41 games, the most in their short team history, but just missed the playoffs. Shaq's trend of making his teams better continued. While LSU faltered in the years after Shaq left, Orlando became a 50-game winner in its fifth season in the NBA and a serious title contender in its sixth.

When it came time for the NBA Draft lottery after Shaq's rookie season, the Magic had a very slim chance at the first pick, but they got it again. Anfernee "Penny" Hardaway was Orlando's second straight number-one pick and he joined Shaq in an inside-outside combination that kept the Magic on the rise.

Shaq had several dominating games in his second season. Two of the most impressive were in New Jersey in November and against Minnesota in April. He scored 24 points, grabbed 28 rebounds, and blocked a career-high 15 shots against the Nets. Late in the season against the Timberwolves, he had 53 points in just 36 minutes.

With Shaq averaging 29.3 points and 13.2 rebounds, the Magic made the playoffs for the first time in 1994.

With Shaq averaging 29.3 points and 13.2 rebounds, the Magic made the playoffs for the first time in 1994. They lost, however, in the first round against the Indiana Pacers.

Shaq averaged 29.3 points per game in the 1994–95 season, leading the league. He also led the league in total points, field goals made, field goals attempted, and free throws attempted while finishing third in rebounding and sixth in blocked shots. This time, when the Magic got to the playoffs, they never stopped until they reached the NBA Finals.

The Magic went 57–25 to win the Atlantic Division and led all Eastern Conference teams in the 1994–95 season. Orlando proved its Eastern Conference superiority by eliminating the Boston Celtics, Chicago Bulls, and Indiana Pacers. The Houston Rockets swept the Magic in four games in the NBA Finals, but Shaq did everything he could to help Orlando's chances by playing 45 minutes per

Michael Jordan and Shaq glare at each other during the fourth quarter of a game in Chicago March 24, 1995.

game and averaging 28 points, 12.5 rebounds, and 2.5 blocked shots in the championship series.

The NBA Championship trophy Shaq talked about after his rookie season would have to wait. He missed 26 games because of injuries and two more to be with his family after his grandmother died during the 1995–96 season. The Magic still managed to increase their win total, going 60–22. Jordan, however, was busy leading the Bulls back to prominence with a 72–10 record.

Once he returned from injury, Shaq worked his way up to third in the league in scoring (26.6 points) and field goal percentage (57.3). The team was ready for the playoffs and eliminated the Detroit Pistons and Atlanta Hawks to get a shot at Chicago. The Bulls made sure the Magic's season ended in a sweep for the third straight season, winning four straight games by a total of 67 points.

CHAPTER SIX

Move 6 to LA

The summer of 1996 featured two major developments in Shaquille O'Neal's career. Shaq enjoyed immediate rewards with his selection to the U.S. Olympic team, which he helped win a gold medal in Atlanta. A decision to sign with the Los Angeles Lakers as a free agent seemed like a natural fit for Shaq and his career interests outside of basketball, but the payoff took longer to receive.

Shaq's presence and the developing career of Kobe Bryant made the Lakers a team that was considered a contender, but they failed to get through the deep Western Conference playoff field in their first three years.

Did it hurt the Orlando Magic to let Shaquille O'Neal get away in the summer of 1996? *Orlando Sentinel* sports writer Tim Povtak seems to think so. An analysis of whether the Magic are cursed, written by Povtak, was the lead story in the *Sentinel* sports section exactly nine years after Shaq signed with the Lakers.

Povtak's analysis started with:

"It was 1996 when Orlando Magic free agent Shaquille O'Neal left for Hollywood, sending this once-charmed franchise tumbling down a rocky, uncertain path, leaving a wake that still ripples almost ten years later.

"It has been the decade of disappointment."

GOLD MEDAL

The Lakers announced the signing of Shaq on July 18, 1996. Before heading for Hollywood, Shaq was needed in Atlanta for the Olympic Games. His signing came a day before the Olympics opened.

DID YOU KNOW?
Shaquille O'Neal made his first appearance with Team USA while helping it to the gold medal in the 1994 World Championships in Toronto, Ontario. The team went undefeated, winning every game by at least 15 points.

Shaq plays for the United States during the Summer Olympic Games in Atlanta in 1996.

Lenny Wilkens, the all-time leader in NBA coaching wins, coached the United States Olympic Team. It was following up on the success of the 1992 Dream Team, which first brought United States professionals to the games. As was the case in 1992, the United States won every game it played on the way to the gold medal, and few were competitive.

Shaq and Penny Hardaway, teammates in Orlando, got one more chance to combine in leading a team to victory. Hardaway scored a team-high 14 points. Shaq added 11 points and 11 rebounds during a 98–75 victory against Brazil in the quarterfinals, the first round of elimination play after the United States swept its pool with five straight wins.

Shaq started three of the eight games and was the team's sixth-leading scorer at 9.3 points per game. He led the United States team with 8 blocked shots. He was second on the team in rebounding with an average of 5.3 and third on the team in field goal percentage at 62.0.

DID YOU KNOW?
The United States won the five games in its pool by an average score of 104–69, including a 133–70 rout of China.

1996 OLYMPIC MEN'S BASKETBALL STANDINGS

Place	Country	Record
1.	United States	8–0
2.	Yugoslavia	7–1
3.	Lithuania	5–3
4.	Australia	5–3
5.	Greece	5–3
6.	Brazil	3–5
7.	Croatia	4–4
8.	China	2–6
9.	Argentina	3–4
10.	Puerto Rico	2–5
11.	Angola	1–6
12.	South Korea	0–7

1996 USA MEN'S OLYMPIC ROSTER

Charles Barkley

Anfernee "Penny" Hardaway

Grant Hill

Karl Malone

Reggie Miller

Hakeem Olajuwon

Shaquille O'Neal

Gary Payton

Scottie Pippen

Mitch Richmond

David Robinson

John Stockton

Head coach: **Lenny Wilkens**

Assistant coaches: **Jerry Sloan, Bobby Cremins, Clem Haskins**

The United States beat Australia, 101–73, in the semifinals before winning the gold medal with a 95–69 romp over Yugoslavia.

ON TO L.A.

Relocating as the prime of his career approached was not a concern for Shaq. "I am a military child," Shaq said that summer. "I'm used to relocating." [1]

Shaq again made an immediate impact with his new team. He averaged 26.2 points and 12.5 rebounds per game, easily making him the only player in the league to average more than 25 points and 10 rebounds. That production led to yet another All-Star Game selection, but Shaq never got to that game.

Injuries wound up disrupting the 1996–97 season for Shaq. He sprained his right ankle in January and then sprained his right knee in early February. As soon as he returned, Shaq suffered a more serious injury, hyperextending his left knee.

The third injury knocked Shaq out of the Lakers' lineup for nearly two months.

As he did whenever injuries knocked him out for part of a season, Shaq got himself ready to return in time for the playoffs. In his first playoff game as a Laker, Shaq scored 46 points against the Portland Trail Blazers. The Lakers reached the second round, where they were eliminated by the Utah Jazz.

Relocating as the prime of his career approached was not a concern for Shaq. "I am a military child, I'm used to relocating."

—Shaquille O'Neal

Shaq had to suffer through two more shortened seasons and two more playoff disappointments as questions grew about whether the Lakers had enough to get to the top.

An abdominal strain caused Shaq to miss more than a month of the 1997–98 season. He returned at the New Year and was back to his productive self as the NBA's Player of the Month for two of the first three calendar months of 1998. In typical Shaq fashion, he led the NBA in field goal percentage, ranked second in scoring, and stood eighth in blocked

Shaq shoots against Utah Jazz center Greg Ostertag in 1997.

shots to be the only player in the league in the top ten in all three categories.

The Lakers went a round further and Shaq scored more than 30 points per game during the playoffs. After beating Portland and the Seattle SuperSonics, the Lakers were swept in four games by Utah in the Western Conference Finals.

Labor problems between the NBA and its players delayed the start of the 1998–99 season and shortened it to 50 games. Shaq scored more points than any other NBA player in the regular season, but the playoffs lasted just two rounds. The Lakers beat the Houston Rockets but were swept by the San Antonio Spurs in the second round.

CHAPTER SEVEN

Shaq's Other Life

7

Shaq already had found fame and fortune on the basketball court, but that did not keep him from enjoying the same rewards in two other professions that he dabbled in off the court. With stardom came endorsements and brief assignments as an actor in commercials.

While in Orlando, Shaq got his first chance to take the giant step in acting, moving from commercials to a movie. Bill Friedkin, the director of *Blue Chips*, a story about college basketball, decided to go with basketball players who could act rather than actors whom they tried to teach to play basketball.

Rapper Master P presents the Athlete of the Year award to Shaq during The Source Hip Hop Awards in 1999.

Shaq, who was coming off his first season with the Magic, and Penny Hardaway, who was about to join the team, were the first players selected for roles in the movie.

Shaq had also put in some time as a rap musician. When he moved his basketball career from Orlando to Los Angeles, the Hollywood scene he was joining just added to the opportunities to venture into movies and music.

> **"I've always wanted to be a rapper even when I was growing up. I wanted to be like Dr. Dre one day. The next day, I wanted to be cool like Run DMC."**
>
> **—Shaquille O'Neal**

Basketball did more than make Shaq famous enough to get a chance to seek new ventures. "I know most rappers and rap fans watch basketball so I kind of throw some basketball in there," he said.[1] Basketball made it into some of his songs, such as "Shoot, Pass, Slam."

"I've always wanted to be a rapper even when I was growing up," Shaq said. "I wanted to be like Dr. Dre one day. The next day, I wanted to be cool like Run DMC."[2]

Shaq had three rap CDs to his credit, along with one completed movie and another being released when he arrived in Los Angeles.

BLUE CHIP

Shaq's worlds converged in *Blue Chips*, starring Nick Nolte as a basketball coach fighting the temptation of taking illegal steps to try to land recruits. Shaq's stepfather had made avoiding such situations an early priority in the recruiting process. A key point in the movie is a game against Indiana, coached by Bobby Knight, the team and coach who ended Shaq's college career.

"I'd done six commercials before the movie, so I was kind of used to being in front of the camera," Shaq said. "To me, acting is facial expression and delivery. I read the script and I liked it. I decided to give it a try."[3]

Playing a basketball player named Neon Boudeaux came easy for Shaq. The on-court scenes looked natural and authentic for a reason. Friedkin filled an Indiana gymnasium with basketball fans and lined up Nolte's Western University Dolphins team against an Indiana team coached by Knight. The game's ending was choreographed, but everything before that was just a case of letting talented

"I'd done six commercials before the movie, so I was kind of used to being in front of the camera. To me, acting is facial expression and delivery. I read the script and I liked it. I decided to give it a try."

—Shaquille O'Neal

**MOVIES FEATURING
SHAQUILLE O'NEAL**

CB4 (1992)

Blue Chips (1993)

Kazaam (1996)

Good Burger (1997)

Steel (1997)

Freddy Got Fingered (2001)

The Wash (2001)

The Kid & I (2005)

basketball players compete against one another with the cameras on and encouraging the fans to react. According to Knight, the teams "played a real game, hard and competitive in front of that crowd, to give Friedkin all the realistic footage he wanted."[4]

Shaq's performance received favorable comments from prestigious reviewers. "O'Neal winds up making the most spectacular play in the film," said *The New York Times.* "He also gives a genuinely appealing performance."[5]

Shaq made an occasional television appearance and starred in more commercials. He also ventured into different roles in later movies. He played a genie in *Kazaam*, a 1996 movie for kids.

RAP IT UP

Both Shaq's on-screen performances and his CD recordings drew mixed reactions. His acting has been mocked at times and some have criticized his dabbling in rap music while being under contract as a basketball star.

But the debut CD, *Shaq Diesel*, went platinum. A review in the *Dallas Morning News* said, "If Shaq chooses to grab the mike full time . . . the transition would be as smooth as a perfectly executed fastbreak."[6]

Shaq followed with five more CDs in the next eight years.

OFFICER SHAQ

Not all of Shaq's outside interests keep him in the spotlight. Shaq has repeatedly shown interest in moving into law enforcement, rather than music and movies, when his basketball career is over. Just as he has done with his higher-profile interests, Shaq has started working on a police career while active as a professional athlete.

In this case, Shaq has avoided the spotlight. After a trade from Los Angeles to Miami in the summer of 2004, Shaq trained to become a Miami Beach reserve officer. He elected a private ceremony in December 2005 when he was sworn in as a reserve so his presence would not distract from the special event for other officers who were being sworn in publicly.

RAP CDS BY SHAQUILLE O'NEAL

Shaq Diesel (1993)

Shaq Fu–Da Return (1994)

The Best of Shaquille O'Neal (1996)

You Can't Stop the Reign (1996)

Respect (1998)

Presents His Superfriends, Volume 1 (2001)

Shaq is sworn in as a reserve police officer in Miami Beach.

Shaq had been a reserve officer for the Los Angeles Port Police after going through the police academy while in Los Angeles. He was named an honorary U.S. deputy marshal and a spokesman for the Safe Surfin' Foundation, which tracks down sexual predators who target children on the Internet.

The training continued in August of 2005 with the Bedford County, Virginia, Sheriff's Office. Shaq went through training on patrolling on land and water as well as investigating cyber crimes.

Shaq says he may run for sheriff in Louisiana or Florida when his playing days are over. "Sheriff is an elective position and I don't just want to be a figurehead," Shaq said. "And I don't want to win because I'm Shaq, but because I have the knowledge and understand what is going on."[7]

8 Breaking Through

Shaquille O'Neal finally got his first professional championship in 2000 with the Los Angeles Lakers. One, however, was not enough. When Shaq celebrated his second straight National Basketball Association title on June 15, 2001, he promised that he was not finished. "I'm happy," Shaq said. ". . . But I'm also greedy, and I'm not done. So I will take a week off, start working out again, come back leaner and meaner and try to get another one next year."[1]

Before the 1999–2000 season, Shaq's college and pro careers had followed similar paths. His teams were clearly better with him than when he was out of the

Shaq yells as he stands behind the NBA Championship trophy during a celebration in Los Angeles June 21, 2000.

lineup. Louisiana State University, the Orlando Magic, and the Los Angeles Lakers were drastically better once he was on the team than they had been before he arrived. Each would also ultimately prove to be significantly weaker after he left.

71

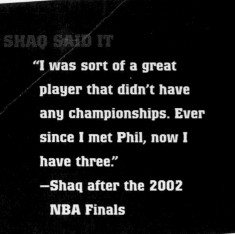

Helping your team win should be the measure of greatness, but Shaq's teams had never won it all. Who could blame him for wanting to prove emphatically that he was indeed a champion? Shaq got his third straight championship in 2002. By then his legacy had changed drastically. There were no questions left about his ability to lead a team to a championship. As had been the case in 2000 and 2001, Shaq was named Most Valuable Player of the NBA Finals. Michael Jordan, often regarded as the best all-around player in league history, is the only other person to be named MVP of three straight NBA Finals. Both Shaq and Jordan won their titles playing for coach Phil Jackson.

FIRST TITLE

Before the Lakers proved they were the best team in the NBA in the 1999–2000 season, Shaq eliminated all doubt about who was the best player. Shaq was the league's leading scorer and second-leading rebounder while finishing third in blocked shots and playing the fourth-most minutes of any player in the NBA.

Shaq holds his MVP trophy while Kobe Bryant carries the NBA Championship trophy as they arrive at an LA airport June 13, 2002.

MULTIPLE WINNERS OF NBA FINALS MVP AWARD

Player	Team(s)	Number	Years
Michael Jordan	Chicago	6	1991–93, 1996–98
Earvin "Magic" Johnson	Los Angeles Lakers	3	1980, 1982, 1987
Shaquille O'Neal	Los Angeles Lakers	3	2000–02
Tim Duncan	San Antonio	3	1999, 2003, 2005
Willis Reed	New York	2	1970, 1973
Kareem Abdul-Jabbar	Milwaukee, Los Angeles Lakers	2	1971, 1985
Larry Bird	Boston	2	1984, 1986
Hakeem Olajuwon	Houston	2	1994, 1995

Before being named MVP of the NBA Finals, he earned MVP awards for the regular season and the All-Star Game. He also won the IBM Award, determined by a computerized rating that measures which player makes the biggest all-around contribution to his team's success. The NBA made Shaq the first player ever to be named Player of the Month three straight times.

From start to finish, Shaq was clearly the best. The Lakers could not be declared the best until they finished what they had started in recent years.

After beating the Sacramento Kings and Phoenix Suns in the first two rounds, the Lakers were stretched to seven games before finally getting past Portland in the Western Conference Finals.

The Trail Blazers appeared ready to put the Lakers away in Game 7. Portland led by fifteen early in the fourth quarter before the Lakers started a frantic comeback. Shaq scored 9 of the Lakers' last 10 points, hitting 5 of 6 foul shots, as the Lakers completed the rally for an 89–84 victory. For the second time in his career and the first time as a Laker, Shaq was leading a team into the NBA Finals.

The Orlando Magic never got a win against the Houston Rockets in their Final. Shaq made sure the Lakers got the early jump on the Indiana Pacers.

2000 NBA FINALS

Game 1 at Los Angeles: Lakers 104, Pacers 87

Game 2 at Los Angeles: Lakers 111, Pacers 104

Game 3 at Indianapolis: Pacers 100, Lakers 91

Game 4 at Indianapolis: Lakers 120, Pacers 118 (overtime)

Game 5 at Indianapolis: Pacers 120, Lakers 87

Game 6 at Los Angeles: Lakers 116, Pacers 111

He broke loose for 43 points and 19 rebounds in the first game. The Lakers held Pacers star Reggie Miller to a 1-for-16 shooting game in a 104–87 romp.

Indiana desperately needed to come up with a way to deal with Shaq. They went to the "Hack-a-Shaq" approach of fouling Shaq before he could make his offensive move and taking their chances that he would miss foul shots. Shaq shot an NBA Finals record 39 foul shots and made just enough (18) to spoil the plan. He scored 40 points and helped the Lakers take a two-game lead with a 111–104 victory.

Kobe Bryant went out with a sprained ankle in Game 2. That allowed Indiana's double-teaming of Shaq, who still scored 33 points, to produce a 100–91 victory in Game 3. The Kobe-Shaq combination was back together for Game 4, and the Lakers again had a two-game lead in the series. Indiana took a 10-point lead on its home court in the fourth game, put together a 21–2 run in the fourth quarter, and got Shaq to foul out in overtime. Bryant made sure none of that mattered in the 120–118 victory.

Indiana, needing to put together a three-game winning streak to take the title, stopped Bryant in Game 5, holding him to 8 points. Shaq had 35 points and 11 rebounds but got little help as the Pacers rolled to a 120–87 rout.

The Lakers returned home with two shots at clinching the title. They only needed one. Indiana led

Shaq defends as the Indiana Pacers' Jalen Rose falls away from the basket in Game 6 of the 2000 NBA Finals.

by five entering the fourth quarter, but the Lakers started with a 15–6 run to take a 94–90 lead. The Pacers rallied to tie once, but the Lakers surged back in front for a 116–111 victory.

"When you're seven-one and you weigh three-thirty-something, you're supposed to be big and strong," Shaq wrote, explaining his tears after winning the first title.

Shaq could be counted on throughout his career to score nearly 30 points per game. In his first chance to lead the Lakers to a title, he averaged 38 points and 16.7 rebounds in the Finals while playing all but three minutes of each game. "The first championship was just to get the monkey off my back," he said.[2]

In Game 6, Shaq played all but one minute and poured in 41 points to make sure the Lakers would be champions. All that was left were the tears and the hugs. Shaq, the unanimous selection as MVP, met family members on the court. He hugged them and lifted them into the air. He cried with joy after winning a championship for the first time in the 11 years since he had been in high school back in San Antonio.

"When you're seven-one and you weigh three-thirty-something, you're supposed to be big and strong," Shaq wrote, explaining his tears after winning the first title. "You are supposed to take whatever people dish out and keep your emotions to yourself. But I needed to let it out. I needed to show people how I was feeling."[3]

BEST RUN EVER

Repeating as champion is often considered to be even tougher than winning for the first time. Teams sometimes have trouble maintaining their motivation.

The 2000–01 Lakers looked sluggish at times early in the season. Shaq took a game off in December to attend graduation ceremonies at LSU, where he had completed his education during the off-season. He missed six games in January and February with a sprained foot.

When Shaq returned from the injury, which also forced him to miss an All-Star Game start, he made it clear that it was time for the team to start driving toward another title. "He came out with a lot of energy post-All-Star break and said, 'Now it's time to start going.' Unfortunately for us, it wasn't time as far as injuries and the scheduling and the things that happened to us," Jackson said. "We weren't able to get ourselves going for another six weeks."[4]

According to Jackson, Shaq made sure the team kept driving. "He kept motivating the team," Jackson said. "He kept his engines going. He kept conditioning and reconditioning himself, taking a lot of time with free throws and all the things that are the

"He kept his engines going. He kept conditioning and reconditioning himself, taking a lot of time with free throws and all the things that are the weak points of his game that he wanted to improve. I think everybody just took his leadership this year as a big plus."

—Phil Jackson

weak points of his game that he wanted to improve. I think everybody just took his leadership this year as a big plus. Shaq, a lot of times, has not been as obvious a leader as he was this year. He truly was a great leader on this team."[5]

Shaq had his usual finish among the league leaders, finishing third in scoring and rebounding and fourth in blocked shots. He was just getting started.

When the Lakers hit the playoffs, they set out on the most dominant postseason run ever. Los Angeles lost just one game while winning 15 for the best playoff record in NBA history.

After the Lakers swept Portland in three games, Shaq scored 44 and 43 in the first two games of a

2001 NBA FINALS

Game One at Los Angeles: 76ers 107, Lakers 101 (overtime)

Game Two at Los Angeles: Lakers 98, 76ers 89

Game Three at Philadelphia: Lakers 96, 76ers 91

Game Four at Philadelphia: Lakers 100, 76ers 86

Game Five at Philadelphia: Lakers 108, 76ers 96

four-game sweep of Sacramento. The Lakers reached the NBA Finals without losing a single game after they also swept San Antonio in the Western Conference Finals.

Shaq's overall playoff average exceeded 30 points for the second straight season, but once again he was at his best during the NBA Finals. When the Lakers reached the Finals, they were on a 19-game winning streak, including the last eight games of the regular season. They suffered their only loss of the playoffs in Game 1 of the NBA Finals, and it took 48 points by Allen Iverson and overtime to put the Lakers away, 107–101. Shaq had 44 points and 20 rebounds in the loss.

The Lakers needed to even the series at home before heading to Philadelphia for three games. They held Iverson to 23 points, less than half his Game 1 output. Shaq scored fewer points, too, but did more of everything else. He had 28 points, 20 rebounds, 9 assists, and 8 blocked shots. The blocked shots total tied Bill Walton, Hakeem Olajuwon, and Patrick Ewing for the most ever in an NBA Finals game.

"Coach wanted me to protect the basket more," Shaq said. "We felt they were getting too many easy shots the first half. So I just tried to step up my defense in the second half."[6] Jackson was pleased with the results. "I thought Shaq was the dramatically better defensive player in this game," he said.[7]

Shaq had 30 points before fouling out late in Game 3. With Shaq gone, frequent Lakers playoff hero Robert Horry scored 7 points in the final minute to preserve a 96–91 victory in Philadelphia and give the Lakers the series lead.

The Lakers took leads and held on in the last two games. Shaq finished the championship series averaging 33 points and 15.8 rebounds while again playing in all but about three minutes per game.

MOST DOMINANT

Shaq had led the Lakers to their first championship. Then he carried them through the best complete playoff run in league history. Other than the championship itself, there were not many ways to make a third title special. Shaq found one. He put together the most dominant offensive effort in Finals history. No player ever scored more than the 145 points Shaq compiled while leading a team to a four-game sweep in the NBA Finals.

The 34 points Shaq scored in completing a sweep of the New Jersey Nets was his lowest output of the playoffs. He scored 36, 40, and 35 points in the first three games of the Finals. The championship was the fourteenth for the Lakers' franchise and the ninth of Coach Jackson's career. It was the first by the Lakers or by Jackson that was captured with a sweep.

NBA FINALS CAREER SCORING LEADERS

Player	Games	Avg.
Rick Barry	10	36.3
Michael Jordan	35	33.6
Jerry West	55	30.5
Shaquille O'Neal	30	28.8
Bob Pettit	25	28.4
Hakeem Olajuwon	17	27.5
Elgin Baylor	44	26.4
Julius Erving	22	25.5
Joe Fulks	11	24.7
Clyde Drexler	15	24.5

Shaq goes up for a basket
in the 2002 NBA Finals.

Shaq led the NBA in field goal percentage for the fifth straight season and was the league's second-leading scorer in the 2001–02 season with a 27.2 points per game average. He played well enough but was a little below his usual playoff numbers as the Lakers eliminated Portland in a three-game sweep and San Antonio, 4–1, in the first two rounds.

When the Lakers faced their strongest challenge of the playoffs against Sacramento in the Western Conference Finals, Shaq's production picked up. He averaged 30.3 points and 13.6 rebounds as the Lakers scraped their way into the Finals.

Once the Lakers reached the Finals, it was clear that New Jersey had no way to stop Shaq. The Nets tried the "Hack-a-Shaq" approach at times. All that accomplished was allowing Shaq to set two more records. He shot well above his career percentage and had the most free throws made (45) and attempted (68) in a four-game NBA Finals series. "I knew if I

2002 NBA FINALS

Game 1 at Los Angeles: Lakers 99, Nets 94

Game 2 at Los Angeles: Lakers 106, Nets 83

Game 3 at East Rutherford, N.J.: Lakers 106, Nets 103

Game 4 at East Rutherford, N.J.: Lakers 113, Nets 107

didn't make my free throws they would go to Hack-a-Shaq, and I didn't want to go through that again," Shaq said.[8]

Shaq also led both teams by averaging 12.3 rebounds per game and was again a unanimous selection for his NBA Finals MVP award. Adding to the excitement of this championship celebration was that it came in New Jersey, just miles from where Shaq was born.

NBA TEAMS WITH THREE OR MORE CONSECUTIVE TITLES		
Minneapolis Lakers	3	1952–54
Boston Celtics	8	1959–66
Chicago Bulls	3	1991–93, 1996–98
Los Angeles Lakers	3	2000–02

CHAPTER NINE

What's in a Name

Only the most special athletes become known strictly by their first names. Having a unique name helps with the recognition. Mention "Shaquille" or "Shaq" to a sports fan and there is no hesitation while wondering who is the subject of the conversation.

Shaq likes to play with his name, altering it into different forms to describe activities in his life, such as "Shaq-A-Claus" to describe his times handing out gifts to underprivileged children. Whatever the context, people know the name is connected to basketball's loveable big man. Shaq uses yet another play on words to describe the charitable foundation he

THE SHAQ DICTIONARY

Hack-a-Shaq: a strategy in which opponents foul Shaq on purpose to make him shoot foul shots

Radio Shaq: an advertising campaign with the electronics store chain Radio Shack

Shaq-A-Claus: a program that Shaq uses to distribute Christmas presents to children at hospitals and other places

Shaq and the Beanstalk—and Other Very Tall Tales: the title of a children's book that Shaq wrote

Shaq Attaq: the title of Shaq's first autobiography

Shaq Diesel: a nickname and the name of his first CD

Shaq Fu: the name of a video game starring the image of Shaq

Shaq Fu: Da Return: the name of one of Shaq's rap albums

Shaq Pack: a program through which he invites under-privileged children to professional games

Shaqsgiving: when Shaq serves the homeless on Thanksgiving

created. Shaq named it the "Real Model Foundation" rather than using the common phrase "role model."

When he's acting in a movie, Shaq plays a role, but he does not like that description when he is devoting time to help his young fans. "Everybody talks about being a role model," Shaq said. "But if you look up the word 'role' in a dictionary, it describes playing a part. Everything I'm into, it's real to me. There's nothing fake about it."[1]

DID YOU KNOW?
Shaquille O'Neal serves as a spokesman for the Reading is Fundamental program.

From his very first season as a professional, Shaq has used significant portions of wealth to provide gifts, food, and other forms of support for those less fortunate. The first step actually took place before he played his first game.

Shaq purchased twenty season tickets to Magic games and gave those tickets to different groups of disadvantaged kids each game. Along with seeing the game, kids received shirts, autographed pictures, and basketball cards. The program has evolved over the years to involve tickets to games in other cities.

Homelessness is not as noticeable a problem in Orlando at it is in some other cities, but it does exist.

Early in his first season, Shaq saw a homeless woman with a sign carrying the message that she would work for food. That got Shaq thinking of ways to help people like her. Shaq had Dennis Tracey, his personal assistant, look into ways to help feed the homeless on Thanksgiving. Tracey called around and found out there were more people needing help than Shaq realized. When he discovered that one shelter would feed about 300 people on Thanksgiving, Shaq hired a catering service to provide food and went over to help serve. Many of the people who received his help that day didn't recognize the big guy serving them a much-needed meal.

DID YOU KNOW?

Shaquille O'Neal wears a size 22 shoe.

HERE COMES SHAQ-A-CLAUS

Shaq-A-Claus started similarly, in Orlando in Shaq's rookie season. What started out as a donation of toys and other items to the Salvation Army led to Shaq receiving a list of needy families, which included nearly 200 kids. It was time for Shaq to get more toys. Shaq, Tracey, and friends could be found at Shaq's house shooting Nerf arrows and water pistols and playing with other toys as they put together packages for the needy. They were not that much older than the people they were helping. "We knew what to buy," Shaq said.

Shaq hands out toys to LA school children in 2001.

> **"We knew what to buy, then we brought it all back to the house and wrapped it ourselves. We knew that was the only way a fifteen-year-old boy wouldn't end up with a Barbie doll or something."**
>
> **—Shaquille O'Neal**

"Then we brought it all back to the house and wrapped it ourselves. We knew that was the only way a fifteen-year-old boy wouldn't end up with a Barbie doll or something."[2] When Shaq distributed the toys days before Christmas with his red Santa cap on, the name Shaq-A-Claus stuck.

Although Shaq did not seek out attention, a few reporters learned about Shaqsgiving and Shaq-A-Claus. Some cynics wondered whether Shaq might be doing such things just for the positive attention.

Shaq received pitches from several worthy causes that sought his involvement. He stuck with situations to which he could relate. Shaq was never homeless, but in the early days back in Newark, times were tough enough that the family occasionally needed the help of food stamps—

a government program that helps provide food for low-income families.

"What I get involved in is what I can see with my own eyes," he said. "Homelessness. Hungry kids. Kids without loving parents. You can think what you want about what I'm involved with, but always remember that I'll be involved. I'll be down there carving the turkey or handing out the presents. That's the only way I could do something without feeling guilty about it."[3]

DID YOU KNOW?
Shaquille O'Neal makes frequent visits to the terminally ill through the Make-A-Wish Foundation.

Like many of his other ideas, Shaq-A-Claus went with Shaq from Orlando to Los Angeles. In Shaq's first season with Miami, he had Shaq-A-Claus events in both Los Angeles and Miami. He took care of his new hometown first. Then, with a Heat-Lakers game scheduled in Los Angeles for Christmas Day, Shaq was able to repeat the event there. He stopped at a Toys R Us and bought many of the gifts himself before arriving at a South Los Angeles Boys & Girls Club in a truck filled with gifts like Sony PlayStations, karaoke machines, bicycles, and sneakers. Because neither city can be pictured as a Winter Wonderland, Shaq brought in fake snow and ice machines to add to the holiday feel.

The support for kids goes well beyond the holidays. Shaq pledged $1 million to the Boys & Girls Clubs of America to support tech-learning centers. "The kids from the places where I grew up can't afford laptops," he said. "When they apply for a job, they'll be far behind."[4]

When kids use the computers to go online, Shaq wants to be sure they are protected. Part of his law enforcement training has been in the area of cyber safety to help learn ways to keep predators away from children online. He is a national spokesman for the Safe Surfin' Foundation. Although he hopes to make it a career someday, much of Shaq's off-season police work is on a volunteer basis.

NEVER STOPS

Shaq's generosity received national media attention during two events in 2005.

Shaq paid for the funeral of another former great Lakers center, George Mikan, who played in the days before stars made the fortunes they do today.

When Hurricane Katrina did so much damage in Louisiana and Mississippi, there were countless people and groups using their fame to help raise the millions of dollars needed for emergencies and long-term rebuilding in the area.

Shaq did more than donate and help raise money. He used his fame and his money to help gather the

Shaq receives a donation from Reina Gual of Miami for Hurricane Katrina victims.

various items needed—food, clothing, medical and sanitary items, and appliances. He arranged for several eighteen-wheelers to carry the items from Florida and Louisiana and traveled along with them.

> **"He's not doing it for publicity. He's doing it because of the kindness of his heart. He's one of the most generous and giving persons I've ever met."**
>
> **—Byron Scott**

Shaq, who rented 400 apartments in the Dallas area for evacuees, was there to thank people who gave donations, and he was there on the other end to encourage the people who so badly needed the help.

Byron Scott, a teammate in Shaq's first season in Los Angeles, was coaching the New Orleans Hornets at the time of the hurricane. He knew firsthand the sincerity of Shaq's efforts and how many more of them have gone unknown to the media and public. "There are so many charities that he gives to, so many things he does for underprivileged kids, so many things he does for families in general that nobody hears about," Scott said. "He's not doing it for publicity. He's doing it because of the kindness of his heart. He's one of the most generous and giving persons I've ever met. And none of it is done for cameras or notoriety. He does it all because that's how he feels; that's how he feels in his heart."[5]

10 Time to Move On

Shaquille O'Neal's college coach, Dale Brown, introduced Shaq to John Wooden, the most successful college coach ever. Wooden had advice for Shaq. The big man carried that advice with him more than a decade later as he prepared to play with new Miami Heat teammate Dwyane Wade for the first time.

Shaq remembers Wooden telling him: "Shaquille, obviously you are a great player, but being great isn't about putting it between your legs, scoring fifty or sixty points. Being great is how you help your other teammates to strive. That is what being great is about."[1]

"Shaquille, obviously you are a great player, but being great isn't about putting it between your legs, scoring fifty or sixty points. Being great is how you help your other teammates to strive."

—John Wooden

During the July 2004 press conference that introduced him as a new member of the Miami Heat, Shaq shared the impression that conversation left on him and how he thought it applied to Wade. "Dwyane had it pretty hard last year because he was a rookie and they started seeing his game," Shaq said. "Now it's going to open up, it's going to open up more room for him. I expect him to be the number one or number two guard in the Eastern Conference because last year he impressed me. I usually don't get impressed by a guard, but he impressed me. Not because of the dunking and all of the stuff that he did, but because he still kept his guys involved and he still did what he did."[2]

Wade responded to Shaq's presence. They formed the type of combination that Hardaway and Shaq had once formed before Bryant and Shaq took the inside-outside, one-two punch to another level. Miami became the best team in the Eastern Conference in the

THEY SAID IT

"Shaq is the greatest center of his time. He's proven that. It took him a while to get to the top. But he worked hard and got to the top and stayed there. That's a testimony to his greatness."

—Kareem Abdul-Jabbar, all-time NBA scoring leader, on ESPN's *SportsCentury* series

2004–05 regular season and came within one game of reaching the NBA Finals. A year later, the Heat was champion of the entire NBA.

Even as the Lakers succeeded in their three-year championship run from 2000 through 2002, there were differences of opinion between Bryant and Shaq. Bryant's legal troubles and the two stars' struggle for the biggest leadership role on the team were distracting at times.

The Lakers made another trip to the NBA Finals in 2004, but it became clear to the organization that one player had to go. The Lakers stuck with the younger Bryant, leaving the three-time Finals MVP free to move on to Miami.

END OF THE RUN

After winning their three straight titles, the Lakers got off to a 4–11 start when Shaq missed the first twelve games of the season after having foot surgery. They eventually climbed into playoff position but went out in the second round of the 2003 playoffs with a loss to the eventual champion San Antonio Spurs.

The 2004 All-Star Game came to Los Angeles. Shaq was again the game's MVP, when he scored 24 points and grabbed 11 rebounds in 24 minutes. The Lakers beat the Houston Rockets, the San Antonio Spurs, and the Minnesota Timberwolves in the Western Conference playoffs to reach the NBA Finals against the Detroit Pistons.

Bryant's three-pointer sent Game 2 of the NBA Finals to overtime. Shaq's dunk fourteen seconds into overtime put the Lakers ahead, and they won, 99–91, to even the series. Facing elimination in Game 5, the Lakers jumped out to a 14–7 lead, but Shaq was called for his second foul and went to the bench. The early

IRREPLACEABLE

Shaq's teams with him in the lineup	656-285	.697
Shaq's teams when he is out of the lineup	99-76	.566

NOTE: Through midway point of 2005–06 season.

Shaq tries to stop the Spurs' Tony Parker during Game 6 of their Western Conference semifinal series May 15, 2003.

momentum got away. The Lakers were behind by 10 at halftime, and their season ended that night. Shaq's stay in Los Angeles ended with it.

LAKERS, BEFORE, DURING, AND AFTER

Before Shaq

1993–94	33–94
1994–95	48–34
1995–96	53–29

With Shaq

1996–97	56–26
1997–98	61–21
1998–99	31–19
1999–2000	67–15
2000–01	56–26
2001–02	58–24
2002–03	50–32
2003–04	56–26

After Shaq

2004–05	34–48
2005–06	45–37

"This summer is going to be a different summer for a lot of people," Shaq said after the loss. "Everyone is going to take care of their own business and everyone is going to do what's best for them, including me."[3] When Lakers general manager Mitch Kupchak made it clear the team intended to rebuild around Bryant, Shaq waited for a trade to be worked out.

NEW START

When Shaq moved to Miami in a trade for three players and a first-round draft pick, an old point was driven home again. The Lakers fell from a team that had won three championships and played in a fourth championship series in five years to one that missed the playoffs in its first year without Shaq. The Heat was the best team in the East for much of the season, but with both Shaq and Wade playing hurt, the team was unable to get past the Pistons in a physical seven-game series.

Shaq played fewer minutes than at any other time in his career. His per game averages of 22.9 points and 10.4 rebounds were well below the best

IMPACT ON HEAT

2002–03, without Shaq	25–57
2003–04, without Shaq	42–40
2004–05, with Shaq	59–23
2005–06, with Shaq	52–30

numbers of his career. Still, his impact in improving the Heat's record by 17 games in the standings was recognized, and Shaq wound up second to Steve Nash of the Phoenix Suns in voting for the Most Valuable Player award. Shaq led the NBA in field goal percentage for the eighth time in his career and hit more than 60 percent of his shots for the first time.

The start of the 2004–05 season saw the Heat win more games than they lost. The team did not take off until December, however, when it won fourteen out of fifteen games. Later in the season, the Heat won eighteen straight games in Miami to set a team record for longest home winning streak.

Shaq sat out two playoff games for the first time in his career because of a deep thigh bruise, but the Heat managed to sweep both the New Jersey Nets and the Washington Wizards to advance to their meeting with the Pistons.

Heat fans made it clear that they recognized Shaq's contributions. While Wade was putting together a 31-point, 15-assist effort in a 108–102 win in Game 2 of the Washington series, the sellout

Shaq looks for an open teammate while being guarded by Rafael Araujo.

crowd chanted "M-V-P" at Shaq. The 15 assists
showed that Wade had learned some of the lessons
Shaq was trying to teach. "It's kind of like pick your
poison," Wade said. "You can either let me shoot or
you can give somebody a layup. And tonight they
came up on me, so other guys got layups."[4] Teams
often face a similar challenge with Shaq: let him
overpower defenders one-on-one inside or double-
team him and give up wide-open jump shots.

Wade suffered a rib injury while the Heat were winning Game 5 to complete a comeback from a 1–0 series deficit to a 3–2 series lead. With the two Heat leaders hurting, the Pistons were able to win the final two games of the series. They eliminated the Heat with an 88–82 victory in Game 7.

MAKING ADJUSTMENTS

The Heat were close to an NBA title, but team president Pat Riley did not sit still after Shaq's first season with the team. Riley, who would return to the bench as coach during the 2005–06 season, traded away Damon Jones and Eddie Jones while adding established players Jason Williams, Antoine Walker, James Posey, and Gary Payton to the lineup. Skeptics wondered if Miami might have too many players who were used to being prominent in their teams' offenses. Shaq had no trouble with the situation.

"I'm not worried at all," he said. "When the general panics, everyone panics."[5] Shaq said he would make sure winning remained the top priority. "First time we get a guy on this team who wants to be a leading scorer or wants to get his picture in the paper, then we're going to be in trouble, we'll all be in trouble. I don't think we'll have that."[6]

Shaq sprained his ankle in the second game of the season and missed 18 games. When he returned, the Heat were just 10–10. By midseason, Miami was up to

CAREER PLAYOFF STATS

Games	194
Minutes Per Game	39.0
Field Goal Percentage	56.6
Free Throw Percentage	50.3
Points Per Game	25.6
Rebounds Per Game	12.2
Assists Per Game	2.8
Blocked Shots Per Game	2.2

second in the Eastern Conference and the new combination was starting to look like another serious title contender. On Martin Luther King Day, Shaq even sought out Bryant, his old teammate, to offer some kind words and to try to bring an end to what had developed into a public feud since Shaq left the Lakers.

The rest of the NBA was noticing the Heat. Shaq, one of the game's all-time greats and a proven clutch performer in championship situations, was once again in position to threaten the league's top teams.

SHAQ'S CAREER HIGHS

STATISTIC	TOTAL	TEAM	OPPONENT	DATE
Points	61	L.A. Lakers	L.A. Clippers	3/6/2000
Field Goals Made	24	L.A. Lakers	L.A. Clippers	3/6/2000
Field Goals Attempted	40	Orlando	Washington	3/22/1996
Free Throws Made	19	L.A. Lakers	Chicago	11/19/1999
Free Throws Attempted	31	L.A. Lakers	Chicago	11/19/1999
Defensive Rebounds	25	L.A. Lakers	Milwaukee	3/21/2004
Total Rebounds	28	Orlando	New Jersey	11/20/1993
Blocked Shots	15	Orlando	New Jersey	11/20/1993
Minutes Played	55	L.A. Lakers	Utah	01/24/2000

BACK ON TOP

Miami kept climbing as the 2005–06 season progressed. The Heat went 23–5 from January 27 through March 29 and coasted to the finish as Southeast Division champions with a 52–30 record, which was second best in the East, behind only Detroit.

Shaq showed he was ready for the start of the playoffs. In the first game, he scored 27 points, grabbed 16 rebounds, and blocked 5 shots to lead the Heat to a 111–106 win against the Chicago Bulls. The Heat finished off the Bulls in six games, with Shaq becoming the first player in franchise history to have at least 20 points and 20 rebounds in one playoff game. He poured in 30 points and ripped down 20 rebounds in the 113–96 road win.

The New Jersey Nets put a little scare into the Heat in the second round. New Jersey opened a 20-point lead after three quarters of the series opener. Even when Shaq returned from foul trouble to score 13 of his 20 points in the fourth quarter, New Jersey held on for a 100–88 victory. The Heat recovered, however, and won four straight games to take the series.

Shaq made sure the Heat had enough to get past the Pistons in the rematch of the disappointing 2004–05 Eastern Conference Finals. Miami went to Detroit and won Game 1, 91–86. After the Pistons tied the series, Shaq put up 27 points and 12 rebounds to lead his team to a 98–83 victory in Game 3. The Heat finished off the Pistons when Shaq hit 12 of 14 shots while scoring 28 points, grabbing 16 rebounds, and blocking 5 shots in a 95–78 romp.

In his press conference after clinching a return trip to the NBA Finals, Riley again pointed to Shaq's role in changing the fortunes of the Heat. "Ever since Shaquille O'Neal showed up on the scene, this team has been a legitimate contender, and we have put pieces around him," Riley said.[7]

Shaq's big effort in Game 6 allowed the Heat to win despite Wade battling the effects of the flu. It also meant the team would not have to win Game 7 in Detroit.

Wade took over from there, leading the team through the championship series with a dominant effort that made him the clear MVP of the NBA Finals. Miami was in serious trouble after losing the first two games in Dallas and falling behind the Mavericks by 13 points in the fourth quarter of Game 3. Wade led the way with 15 points in the fourth quarter, rallying the Heat to a 98–96 victory. Wade averaged 40.3 points in three straight home wins, then scored 36 in the clincher, a 95–92 victory in Dallas.

"I came to Miami because of this young fella right here," O'Neal said while joining Wade for the trophy presentation. "I thought he was a special player. I knew the first time I saw him, I knew he was something special, so I knew it was my job to come here and make him better."[8]

Shaq still played a significant role. He sat on the bench through the fourth quarter of the Game 2 loss after managing just 5 points and 6 rebounds in the worst playoff effort of his career. Shaq came back to grab at least 11 rebounds in each of the remaining four games. He had 17 points in the win that tied the series and 18 in a 101–100 overtime victory to put Miami ahead by a game.

The fear of what Shaq might do in the middle helped open up outside shots and driving lanes for Wade. "Everything starts with Shaq, really," Dirk Nowitzki, the Mavericks' MVP candidate, said. "The way he's dominant in the post, it opens up everything for the outside guys. If you don't double team him, he's just going to walk you under the basket and score every time. So he kind of makes you scramble and rotate all over the place. . . . He's still the most dominant player in the league."[9]

2006 NBA FINALS

Game 1 at Dallas: Mavericks 90, Heat 80

Game 2 at Dallas: Mavericks 99, Heat 85

Game 3 at Miami: Heat 98, Mavericks 96

Game 4 at Miami: Heat 98, Mavericks 74

Game 5 at Miami: Heat 101, Mavericks 100 (overtime)

Game 6 at Dallas: Heat 95, Mavericks 92

CAREER STATISTICS

YEAR	TEAM	G	MIN	FGM-A	FG%	FTM-A
92–93	Orlando	81	3,071	733–1,304	0.562	427–721
93–94	Orlando	81	3,224	953–1,591	0.599	471–850
94–95	Orlando	79	2,923	930–1,594	0.583	455–854
95–96	Orlando	54	1,946	592–1,033	0.573	249–511
96–97	LA Lakers	51	1,941	552–991	0.557	232–479
97–98	LA Lakers	60	2,175	670–1,147	0.584	359–681
98–99	LA Lakers	49	1,705	510–885	0.576	269–498
99–00	LA Lakers	79	3,163	956–1,665	0.574	432–824
00–01	LA Lakers	74	2,924	813–1,422	0.572	499–972
01–02	LA Lakers	67	2,422	712–1,229	0.579	398–717
02–03	LA Lakers	67	2,535	695–1,211	0.574	451–725
03–04	LA Lakers	67	2,464	554–948	0.584	331–676
04–05	Miami	73	2,492	658–1,095	0.601	353–765
05–06	Miami	59	1,806	480–800	0.600	221–471
Career		941	34,791	9,808–16,915	0.580	5,147–9,744

KEY:
G = Games Played
MIN = Minutes Played
FGM-A = Field Goals Made-Attempted
FG% = Field Goal Percentage
FTM-A = Free Throws Made-Attempted
FT% = Free Throw Percentage
REB = Rebounds
AST = Assists
STL = Steals
BLK = Blocked Shots
PTS = Points Scored
AVG = Points Per Game Average

FT%	REB	AST	STL	BLK	PTS	AVG
0.592	1,122	152	60	286	1,893	23.4
0.554	1,072	195	76	231	2,377	29.3
0.533	901	214	73	192	2,315	29.3
0.487	596	155	34	115	1,434	26.6
0.484	640	159	46	147	1,336	26.2
0.527	681	142	39	144	1,699	28.3
0.540	525	114	36	82	1,289	26.3
0.524	1,078	299	36	239	2,344	29.7
0.513	940	277	47	204	2,125	28.7
0.555	715	200	41	137	1,822	27.2
0.622	742	206	38	159	1,841	27.5
0.490	769	196	34	166	1,439	21.5
0.461	760	200	36	171	1,669	22.9
0.469	541	113	23	104	1,181	20.0
0.528	11,082	2,622	619	2,377	24,764	26.3

CAREER ACHIEVEMENTS

1989 State high school championship at Cole High School, San Antonio, Texas

1990–91 Led National Collegiate Athletic Association Division I players in rebounds

1990–91 Named College Basketball Player of the Year by The Associated Press, United Press International, and *Sports Illustrated*

1991–92 Led NCAA Division I players in blocked shots

1991–92 First-team All-American

1992 First player selected in National Basketball Association Draft

1992–93 NBA Rookie of the Year

1994 Helped Team USA win World Basketball Championships

1994–95 Led NBA in scoring with an average of 29.3 points per game

1996 Youngest player selected on the NBA's 50 Greatest Players in History

July 1996	Won gold medal with Team USA in Olympics
1999–2000	Led NBA in scoring with an average of 29.7 points per game
1999–2000	Named Most Valuable Player of NBA regular season, NBA All-Star Game, and NBA Finals where he led Los Angeles Lakers to title
June 2001	Named MVP of the NBA Finals while helping Lakers to second straight title
June 2002	Named MVP of the NBA Finals while helping Lakers to third straight title
2004	Named MVP of NBA All-Star Game
2004–05	Runner-up in voting for NBA MVP award
2005–06	Wins fourth NBA title and first since joining Miami Heat

CHAPTER NOTES

CHAPTER 1. HAPPY IN MIAMI

1. <http://www.entrepreneur.com/article/0,4621,323614,00.html> (December 23, 2005).

2. *Milwaukee Journal Sentinel*, February 15, 2005, <http://www.jsonline.com/sports/buck/feb05/302023.asp> (December 23, 2005).

3. Liz Robbins, "As the heat rises, O'Neal stays cool to lead the troops," *The New York Times*, October 31, 2005.

4. *Milwaukee Journal Sentinel*, February 15, 2005, <http://www.jsonline.com/sports/buck/feb05/302023.asp> (December 23, 2005).

CHAPTER 2. MOVING HERE AND THERE

1. Shaquille O'Neal, with Jack McCallum, *Shaq Attaq!* (New York: Hyperion: 1994), p. 23.

2. Ibid.

3. Ibid.

4. Ibid., p. 73.

5. Ibid., p. 22.

CHAPTER 3. GROWING UP SHAQ

1. David Flores, "Shaq challenged daily by former Cole coach," *San Antonio Express-News*, March 5, 2004, <http://www.mysanantonio.com/sports /hss-ports/stories/MYSA05.01C.David_Flores_column_03050.3440eec9.html> (December 31, 2005).

2. Ibid.

3. Ibid.

4. Shaquille O'Neal, with Jack McCallum, *Shaq Attaq!* (New York: Hyperion: 1994), p. 146.

5. David Flores, "Shaq challenged daily by former Cole coach," *San Antonio Express-News*, March 5, 2004, <http://www.mysanantonio.com/sports/ hss-ports/stories/MYSA05.01C.David_Flores_column_03050.3440eec9.html> (December 31, 2005).

6. Shaquille O'Neal, with Jack McCallum, *Shaq Attaq!* (New York: Hyperion: 1994), p. 144.

7. David Flores, "Shaq challenged daily by former Cole coach," *San Antonio Express-News*, March 5, 2004, <http://www.mysanantonio.com/sports/ hss-ports/stories/MYSA05.01C.David_Flores_column_03050.3440eec9.html> (December 31, 2005).

8. Shaquille O'Neal, with Jack McCallum, *Shaq Attaq*! (New York: Hyperion: 1994), p. 143.

CHAPTER 4. SHAQ THE TIGER

1. Shaquille O'Neal, with Jack McCallum, *Shaq Attaq!* (New York: Hyperion: 1994), p. 164.

2. Ibid., p. 165.

CHAPTER 5. MAGIC TIMES

1. Associated Press report, "O'Neal Joins the Magic For Reported $40 Million," *The New York Times*, August 8, 1992, <http://select.nytimes.com/ gst/abstract.html?res=F1061EFD3B5A0C7B8CDDA10894DA494D81&n=Top% 2fReference%2fTimes%20Topics%2fPeople%2fO%2fO%27Neal%2c%20Sh aquille> (January 23, 2006).

2. Associated Press report, "SPORTS PEOPLE: BASKETBALL; No. 1 Decides on No. 32," *The New York Times*, August 26, 1992, <http://query.nytimes.com/ gst/fullpage.html?res=9E0CE3D9173AF935A1575BC0A964958260&n=Top%2 fReference%2fTimes%20Topics%2fPeople%2fO%2fO%27Neal%2c%20Sha quille> (January 23, 2006).

3. Associated Press report, "O'Neal Shatters Rookie Vote," *The New York Times,* May 7, 1993, <http://query.nytimes.com/gst/fullpage.html? res=9F0CE1D9163DF934A35756C0A965958260&n=Top%2fReference%2fTim es%20Topics%2fPeople%2fO%2fO%27Neal%2c%20Shaquille> (January 23, 2006).

CHAPTER 6. MOVE TO LA

1. Bill Saporito with Mark Thompson, "STARS' SALARIES: SWISH!, A Run of Huge Contracts Gives the Top Players a Taller Portion of the N.B.A.'s Ever Richer Revenues," *TIME Magazine*, Volume 148, No. 6, July 29, 1996.

CHAPTER 7. SHAQ'S OTHER LIFE

1. Clarence Waldron, "Shaquille O'Neal talks about basketball, his hit album and a movie deal," *Jet Magazine*, May 16, 1994, COPYRIGHT 1994 Johnson Publishing Co. COPYRIGHT 2004 Gale Group, <http://www.findarticles. com/p/articles/mi_m1355/is_n2_v86/ai_15456267> (January 23, 2006).

2. Ibid.

3. Ibid.

4. Bob Knight, with Bob Hammel, *Knight: My Story* (New York: St. Martin's Griffin, 2002).

5. Rebecca Mead, *The New Yorker,* May 20, 2002, <http://www.rebeccamead. com/2002/2002_05_20_art_shaq.htm> (January 23, 2006).

6. Sean Piccoli, "Shaq the Rapper," *Florida Sun-Sentinel,* July 21, 2004, <http://www.sun-sentinel.com/sports/ basketball/heat/shaq/sfl-shaqflixn-raps21jul21,0,6082650.story?coll=sfla-shaq-headlines> (January 23, 2006).

7. Rebecca Mead, *The New Yorker,* May 20, 2002. <http://www.rebeccamead. com/2002/2002_05_20_art_shaq.htm> (January 23, 2006).

CHAPTER 8. BREAKING THROUGH

1. Finals quotes, NBA Web site, <http://aol.nba.com/finals2001/ quotes_index.html?nav=ArticleList> (January 24, 2006).

2. NBA Web site, <http://aol.nba.com/finals2001/quotes_lakers_ 010615.html?nav=ArticleList> (January 24, 2006).

3. Shaquille O'Neal, *Shaq Talks Back,* (New York: St. Martin's Press, 2001) p. 1.

4. NBA Web site, <http://aol.nba.com/finals2001/quotes_lakers_ 010615.html?nav=ArticleList> (January 24, 2006).

5. Ibid.

6. SportsTicker, *CNNSI.com* Web site.<http://sportsillustrated.cnn.com/ basketball/nba/ recaps/2001/06/08/lal_phi/> (January 24, 2006).

7. Ibid.

8. Associated Press report, "Good company: Shaq, MJ only players to win three straight Finals MVPs," *Sports Illustrated* Web site, June 13, 2002, <http://sportsillustrated.cnn.com/basketball/nba/2002/playoffs/news/ 2002/06/12/shaq_mvp_ap/> (January 24, 2006).

CHAPTER 9. WHAT'S IN A NAME

1. Ethan Skolnick and Dennis McCafferty, "Our '05 Most Caring Athletes," *USA Weekend,* <http://www.usaweekend.com/05_issues/ 050925/050925mcc.html> (January 26, 2006).

2. Shaquille O'Neal, with Jack McCallum, *Shaq Attaq!* (New York: Hyperion: 1994), p. 104.

3. Ibid., pp. 104–105.

4. Ethan Skolnick and Dennis McCafferty, "Our '05 Most Caring Athletes," *USA Weekend,* <http://www.usaweekend.com/05_issues/050925/ 050925mcc.html> (January 26, 2006).

5. Jimmy Smith, "Still Lovin' Shaq: O'Neal continues to make friends everywhere he goes," *New Orleans Times-Picayune,* October 25, 2005, <http://www.nola.com/sports/t-p/index.ssf?/base/sports-20/1130221456302410.xml> (January 26, 2006).

CHAPTER 10. TIME TO MOVE ON

1. The Sports Network, July 28, 2004, <http://www.sportsnetwork.com/default.asp?c=sportsnetwork&page=nba/misc/blatt_archive/beyond_072804.htm> (January 25, 2006).

2. The Sports Network, July 28, 2004, <http://www.sportsnetwork.com/default.asp?c=sportsnetwork&page=nba/misc/blatt_archive/beyond_072804.htm> (January 25, 2006).

3. Compiled by Ira Winderman, "Speaking of Shaq ...," *Florida Sun-Sentinel,* July 11, 2004, <http://www.sun-sentinel.com/sports/basketball/heat/sfl-shaqquote11jul11,0,3580724.story?coll=sfla-sports-utility-shaq> (January 25, 2006).

4. Associated Press report, "HEAT 108, WIZARDS 102: The guard scores 31, including a crucial three-pointer, and dishes out a career-high 15 assists," *St. Petersburg Times,* May 11, 2005, <http://www.sptimes.com/2005/05/11/Sports/Wade_key_in_keeping_t.shtml> (January 25, 2006).

5. Liz Robbins, "As the heat rises, O'Neal stays cool to lead the troops," *The New York Times,* October 31, 2005.

6. Ibid.

7. Miami Heat playoff Web site, June 2, 2006, http://aol.nba.com/heat/chat/quotes_060602.html (June 25, 2006).

8. Transcript of NBA Finals Trophy Presentation. http://noticias.info/asp/aspcomunicados.asp?nid=191916 (June 25, 2006).

9. Miami Heat playoff Web site, June 20, 2006, http://aol.nba.com/heat/chat/quotes_060620.html (June 25, 2006).

GLOSSARY

actor—A person who performs in a movie.

assist—A pass that leads to a basket.

charity—The act of giving or an organization that gives to the needy.

contract—A written agreement between a player and a team stating how long the player is expected to be part of the team and how much he will be paid.

director—A person who organizes a movie, instructing the actors, cameramen, etc.

draft—A process in which professional sports teams choose players in order.

field goal—A basket made while the clock is running in basketball; any shot other than a foul shot.

free throw—Also known as a foul shot; attempts given to teams after a foul or technical foul has been called.

Olympics—A sporting competition pitting teams from different countries against one another in multiple sports.

rebound—To gain possession of the basketball after a missed shot.

rookie—A first-year professional.

scholarship—A grant of money to a student for educational purposes; top athletes are offered scholarships by colleges to attend and play sports for their schools.

playoffs—A series of games between two teams to eliminate the losing team and send the winning team on to another round until just one team remains as the champion.

post—To establish a position near the basket.

FOR MORE INFORMATION

FURTHER READING

Bernstein, Ross. *Shaquille O'Neal*. Minneapolis: LernerSports, 2005.

Christian, Charlie. *Shaquille O'Neal*. New York: Barnes & Noble Books, 2003.

O'Neal, Shaquille. *Shaq and the Beanstalk and Other Very Tall Tales*. New York: Scholastic, 1999.

O'Neal, Shaquille, with Jack McCallum. *Shaq Attaq!*. New York: Hyperion Books, 1993.

WEB LINKS

Shaq's player page on NBA Web site
http://aol.nba.com/playerfile/shaquille_oneal/index.html?nav=page

Shaq's player page at Basketball-Reference.com
http://www.basketball-reference.com/players/o/onealsh01.html

LSU Athletics' Web site
http://www.lsusports.net/ViewArticle.dbml?DB_OEM_ID=5200&ATCLID=174841

INDEX

O

W